foundations

SMALL GROUP STUDY GUIDE

taught by tom Holladay and kay warren

GOOD AND EVIL

 ZONDERVAN®    SADDLEBACK CHURCH

ZONDERVAN.com/
AUTHORTRACKER
follow your favorite authors

Foundations: *Good and Evil Study Guide*
Copyright © 2003, 2004, 2008 by Tom Holladay and Kay Warren

Requests for information should be addressed to:
Zondervan, *Grand Rapids, Michigan* 49530

ISBN 978-0-310-27687-6

08 09 10 11 12 13 14 15 16 17 18 • 23 22 21 20 19 18 17 16 15 14 13 12 11 10 9 8 7 6 5 4 3 2 1

foundations TABLE OF CONTENTS

FOREWORD

What *Foundations* Will Do for You

I once built a log cabin in the Sierra Mountains of northern California. After ten backbreaking weeks of clearing forest land, all I had to show for my effort was a leveled and squared concrete foundation. I was discouraged, but my father, who built over a hundred church buildings in his lifetime, said, "Cheer up, son! Once you've laid the foundation, the most important work is behind you." I've since learned that this is a principle for all of life: you can never build *anything* larger than the foundation can handle.

The foundation of any building determines both its size and strength, and the same is true of our lives. A life built on a false or faulty foundation will never reach the height that God intends for it to reach. If you skimp on your foundation, you limit your life.

That's why this material is so vitally important. *Foundations* is the biblical basis of a purpose-driven life. You must understand these life-changing truths to enjoy God's purposes for you. This curriculum has been taught, tested, and refined over ten years with thousands of people at Saddleback Church. I've often said that *Foundations* is the most important class in our church.

Why You Need a Biblical Foundation for Life

- *It's the source of personal growth and stability.* So many of the problems in our lives are caused by faulty thinking. That's why Jesus said the truth will set us free and why Colossians 2:7a (CEV) says, *"Plant your roots in Christ and let him be the foundation for your life."*

- *It's the underpinning of a healthy family.* Proverbs 24:3 (TEV) says, *"Homes are built on the foundation of wisdom and understanding."* In a world that is constantly changing, strong families are based on God's unchanging truth.

- *It's the starting point of leadership.* You can never lead people farther than you've gone yourself. Proverbs 16:12b (MSG) says, *"Sound leadership has a moral foundation."*

- *It's the basis for your eternal reward in heaven.* Paul said, *"Whatever we build on that foundation will be tested by fire on the day of judgment . . . We will be rewarded if our building is left standing"* (1 Corinthians 3:12, 14 CEV).

- *God's truth is the only foundation that will last.* The Bible tells us that *"the sound, wholesome teachings of the Lord Jesus Christ . . . are the foundation for a godly life"* (1 Timothy 6:3 NLT), and that *"God's truth stands firm like a foundation stone . . ."* (2 Timothy 2:19 NLT).

Jesus concluded his Sermon on the Mount with a story illustrating this important truth. Two houses were built on different foundations. The house built on sand was destroyed when rain, floods, and wind swept it away. But the house built on the foundation of solid rock remained firm. He concluded, *"Therefore everyone who hears these words of mine and puts them into practice is like a wise man who built his house on the rock"* (Matthew 7:24 NIV). *The Message* paraphrase of this verse shows how important this is: *"These words I speak to you are not incidental additions to your life . . . They are foundational words, words to build a life on."*

I cannot recommend this curriculum more highly to you. It has changed our church, our staff, and thousands of lives. For too long, too many have thought of theology as something that doesn't relate to our everyday lives, but *Foundations* explodes that mold. This study makes it clear that the foundation of what we do and say in each day of our lives is what we believe. I am thrilled that this in-depth, life-changing curriculum is now being made available for everyone to use.

— Rick Warren, author of *The Purpose Driven® Life*

PREFACE

Get ready for a radical statement, a pronouncement sure to make you wonder if we've lost our grip on reality: *There is nothing more exciting than doctrine!*

Track with us for a second on this. Doctrine is the study of what God has to say. What God has to say is always the truth. The truth gives me the right perspective on myself and on the world around me. The right perspective results in decisions of faith and experiences of joy. *That* is exciting!

The objective of *Foundations* is to present the basic truths of the Christian faith in a simple, systematic, and life-changing way—in other words, to teach doctrine. The question is, why? In a world in which people's lives are filled with crying needs, why teach doctrine? Because biblical doctrine has the answer to many of those crying needs! Please don't see this as a clash between needs-oriented and doctrine-oriented teaching. The truth is we need both. We all need to learn how to deal with worry in our lives. One of the keys to dealing with worry is an understanding of the biblical doctrine of the hope of heaven. Couples need to know what the Bible says about how to have a better marriage. They also need a deeper understanding of the doctrine of the Fatherhood of God, giving the assurance of God's love upon which all healthy relationships are built. Parents need to understand the Bible's practical insights for raising kids. They also need an understanding of the sovereignty of God, a certainty of the fact that God is in control, that will carry them through the inevitable ups and downs of being a parent. Doctrinal truth meets our deepest needs.

Welcome to a study that will have a lifelong impact on the way you look at everything around you and above you and within you. Helping you develop a "Christian worldview" is our goal as the writers of this study. A Christian worldview is the ability to see everything through the filter of God's truth. The time you dedicate to this study will lay a foundation for new perspectives that will have tremendous benefits for the rest of your life. This study will help you:

- Lessen the stress in everyday life
- See the real potential for growth the Lord has given you
- Increase your sense of security in an often troubling world
- Find new tools for helping others (your friends, your family, your children) find the right perspective on life
- Fall more deeply in love with the Lord

Throughout this study you'll see three types of sidebar sections designed to help you connect with the truths God tells us about himself, ourselves, and this world.

- *A Closer Look:* We'll take time to expand on a truth or look at it from a different perspective.

- *A Fresh Word:* One aspect of doctrine that makes people nervous is the "big words." Throughout this study we'll take a fresh look at these words, words like *omnipotent* and *sovereign*.

- *Key Personal Perspective:* The truth of doctrine always has a profound impact on our lives. In this section we'll focus on that personal impact.

- *Living on Purpose:* James 1:22 (NCV) says, *"Do what God's teaching says; when you only listen and do nothing, you are fooling yourselves."* In his book, *The Purpose Driven Life,* Rick Warren identifies God's five purposes for our lives. They are worship, fellowship, discipleship, ministry, and evangelism. We will focus on one of these five purposes in each lesson, and discuss how it relates to the subject of the study. This section is very important, so please be sure to leave time for it.

Here is a brief explanation of the other features of this study guide.

Looking Ahead/Catching Up: You will open each meeting with an opportunity for everyone to check in with each other about how you are doing with the weekly assignments. Accountability is a key to success in this study!

Key Verse: Each week you will find a key verse or Scripture passage for your group to read together. If someone in the group has a different translation, ask them to read it aloud so the group can get a bigger picture of the meaning of the passage.

Video Lesson: There is a video lesson segment for the group to watch together each week. Take notes in the lesson outlines as you watch the video, and be sure to refer back to these notes during your discussion time.

Discovery Questions: Each video segment is complemented by questions for group discussion. Please don't feel pressured to discuss every single question. The material in this study is meant to be your servant, not your master, so there is no reason to rush through the answers. Give everyone ample opportunity to share their thoughts. If you don't get through all of the discovery questions, that's okay.

Prayer Direction: At the end of each session you will find suggestions for your group prayer time. Praying together is one of the greatest privileges of small group life. Please don't take it for granted.

Get ready for God to do incredible things in your life as you begin the adventure of learning more deeply about the most exciting message in the world: the truth about God!

— Tom Holladay and Kay Warren

HOW TO USE THIS VIDEO CURRICULUM

Here is a brief explanation of the features on your small group DVD. These features include a *Group Lifter,* four *Video Teaching Sessions* by Tom Holladay and Kay Warren and a short video, *How to Become a Follower of Jesus Christ,* by Rick Warren. Here's how they work:

The Group Lifter is a brief video introduction by Tom Holladay giving you a sense of the objectives and purpose of this *Foundations* study on good and evil. Watch it together as a group at the beginning of your first session.

The Video Teaching Sessions provide you with the teaching for each week of the study. Watch these features with your group. After watching the video teaching session, continue in your study by working through the discussion questions and activities in the study guide.

Nothing is more important than the decision you make to accept Jesus Christ as your Lord and Savior. You will have the option to watch a short video presentation, *How to Become a Follower of Jesus Christ,* at the end of Session Two. In this brief video segment, Rick Warren explains the importance of having Christ as the Savior of your life and how you can become part of the family of God. If everyone in your group is already a follower of Christ, or if you feel there is a better time to play this segment, continue your session by turning to the Discovery Questions in your DVD study guide. You can also select this video presentation separately on the Main Menu of the DVD for viewing at any time.

Follow these simple steps for a successful small group session:

1. Hosts: Watch the video session and write down your answers to the discussion questions in the study guide before your group arrives.

2. Group: Open your group meeting by using the "Looking Ahead" or "Catching Up" section of your lesson.

3. Group: Watch the video teaching lesson and follow along in the outlines in the study guide.

4. Group: Complete the rest of the discussion materials for each session in the study guide.

It's just that simple. Have a great study together!

1

WHY EVIL EXISTS

LOOKING AHEAD

When you hear the word "evil," what picture, person, historical event, or circumstance comes to mind?

Key Verse

For the LORD is good and his love endures forever;
his faithfulness continues through all generations.

Psalm 100:5 (NIV)

BIBLE TEACHING
Watch the video lesson now and take notes in your outline on pages 3–5.

Why Does Evil Exist in God's World?

Three Truths

1. God is _____ .

   - His _____ is good.

     For the LORD is good and his love endures forever; his faithfulness continues through all generations.
     (Psalm 100:5 NIV)

   - His _____ are good.

     God saw all that he had made, and it was very good.
     (Genesis 1:31a NIV)

2. God is _____ .

   Great and powerful God, your name is the LORD All-Powerful.
   (Jeremiah 32:18b NCV)

3. The world is _____ .

   "Their sentence is based on this fact: that the Light from heaven came into the world, but they loved the darkness more than the Light, for their deeds were evil." (John 3:19 LB)

   Stop loving this evil world and all that it offers you . . .
   (1 John 2:15 LB)

How can these be true?

How could a good and all-powerful God create a world in which evil could exist and continues to exist? A lot of theological and philosophical jargon can be summed up in one simple sentence:

> There is no _____ without choice.

God could have made a person who would never have chosen to sin, but then that person would have been denied the opportunity to choose to love.

Two Truths to Remember:

1) God is _____ .

2) Mankind has _____ choice.

How do you reconcile these two? If God gives us choice, doesn't that put us in control rather than him? Our God is able to give us, as a part of his creation, a free will to decide and yet remain in complete control of his creation. How does he do that? He is God!

Be sure to keep these two truths in balance. If you lean too far toward God's being in control, you come down on the side of fatalism: it doesn't matter what we do. If you lean too far toward man's free will, you come down on the side of humanism: we are in control of our fate.

Three Reasons Evil Exists

1. God's will: because God _____ evil.

The problem of evil and suffering is possibly the single greatest intellectual challenge to Christianity. It's hard for people to understand how a great and good God could allow evil to exist.

- He made a world in which evil _____ exist.

- God allows evil to _____ to exist.

  So I gave them over to their stubborn hearts to follow their own devices. (Psalm 81:12 NIV)

A CLOSER LOOK

God's Response to Suffering

The fact that God allows suffering does not mean he enjoys suffering.

1. He directly _____ some suffering. He is the punisher of evil. (Isaiah 13:11)

2. He has _____ for all suffering. (2 Corinthians 1:3–4; Lamentations 3:22–23; Matthew 14:14)

3. He is willing to _____ for us in our suffering. (Psalm 46:1; Hebrews 4:16)

4. He develops our _____ through suffering. (James 1:2–4; Hebrews 2:10)

5. He will one day _____ all suffering. (Revelation 21:3–4; Romans 8:18)

DISCOVERY QUESTIONS

1. Why do you think it's important to be honest about the fact that we live in an evil world? What happens when we deny the reality of evil?

2. What are some ways we can show compassion for those who are suffering?

3. Several of you share an example of how you have seen your character develop as a result of a time of suffering.

4. What gives you the greatest hope and encouragement as you face personal suffering?

Did You Get It? How has this week's study helped you see the truth of the reality of evil?

Share with Someone: Think of a person you can encourage with the truth you learned in this session. Write their name in the space below and pray for God to provide that opportunity this week.

LIVING ON PURPOSE
Fellowship
Is there someone in your group who is currently going through a season of suffering? What can you do as a group to help them?

PRAYER DIRECTION

Focus together in prayer on God's immeasurable power. Praise him for the fact that his power is available as you battle evil in this world.

NOTES

Session two

2

SATAN'S INFLUENCE— MAN'S CHOICE

CATCHING UP

1. Who did you share last week's truth with?

2. Did you find your faith being strengthened this last week as you encouraged someone else who is facing a time of suffering?

Key Verse

... for all have sinned and fall short of the glory of God ...

Romans 3:23 (NIV)

BIBLE TEACHING

Watch the video lesson now and take notes in your outline on pages 11–13.

Three Reasons Evil Exists (continued)

1. God's will: he allows evil.

2. Satan's influence: because Satan _____ evil.

Evil is not some new creation of Satan—Satan does not have the power to create anything. All he can do is try to twist or withhold what God has created.

Satan: a brief biography

- He was an _____ in heaven. (Revelation 12:3–9; 9:11)

- He _____ from heaven due to pride. (Revelation 12:7–9; Isaiah 14:12–15)

- He has been given _____ freedom to influence the earth.

  Satan's limit: he must ask _____ .

  "... Have you considered my servant Job? There is no one on earth like him; he is blameless and upright, a man who fears God and shuns evil." (Job 1:8 NIV)

- He is unalterably _____ to eternal destruction.

  And the devil, who deceived them, was thrown into the lake of burning sulfur ... (Revelation 20:10 NIV)

3. Mankind's choice: because we _____ evil.

Evil began with _____ . (Genesis 3)

Adam and Eve passed along to us as their children a sin nature.
Sin became a part of all of us when they bit into the forbidden fruit
in the garden of Eden. That's why we all inevitably sin. We cannot
refuse the temptation of evil. That is called "original sin." We don't
start with a clean slate. We all start with the knowledge of good and
of evil and with a flawed heart that causes us to sin.

> *Therefore, just as sin entered the world through one man, and
> death through sin, and in this way death came to all men,
> because all sinned . . .* (Romans 5:12 NIV)

Evil is present in _____ .

It's not just "their fault." We must all admit that "evil is present
in me."

> *. . . When I want to do good, evil is right there with me.*
> (Romans 7:21 NIV)

> [9]*What shall we conclude then? Are we any better? Not at all!
> We have already made the charge that Jews and Gentiles alike
> are all under sin.* [10]*As it is written: "There is no one righteous,
> not even one;* [11]*there is no one who understands, no one who
> seeks God.* [12]*All have turned away, they have together become
> worthless; there is no one who does good, not even one."*
> (Romans 3:9–12 NIV)

Why does God continue to allow evil?

- He already has _____ evil.

  > *In this way, God disarmed the evil rulers and authorities. He
  > shamed them publicly by his victory over them on the cross of
  > Christ.* (Colossians 2:15 NLT)

- He is _____.

The Lord is not slow in keeping his promise, as some understand slowness. He is patient with you, not wanting anyone to perish, but everyone to come to repentance.
(2 Peter 3:9 NIV)

KEY PERSONAL PERSPECTIVE
Why does God allow bad things to happen?

How do you answer someone when they ask you a question like: "How could a perfect, good, and all-powerful God allow wars and disease in the world today?" When faced with tragedy our first impulse is to ask, "Why? Why would God allow this to happen?" The study has reminded us of some of the answers, for ourselves and for others.

1. The world is evil, not because of God's creation, but because of mankind's choice.

2. God cares about those who suffer.

3. It is God's proclaimed purpose to one day do away with evil.

4. The reason he waits is so more people might be saved, therefore not having to suffer eternal separation from him.

"HOW TO BECOME A FOLLOWER OF JESUS CHRIST"

Have you ever surrendered your life to Jesus Christ? Take a few minutes with your group to watch a brief video by Pastor Rick Warren on how to become part of the family of God. It is included on the Main Menu of this DVD.

DISCOVERY QUESTIONS

1. What are some ways we tend to "place blame" when we encounter evil? Why is it unhealthy to always blame someone else for the evil in the world?

2. How has faith in God replaced your fears of Satan and evil?

3. How can the knowledge of God's ultimate victory over evil influence you to act differently this week?

4. Jesus taught us to pray *"deliver us from evil"* (Matthew 6:13 KJV). In what circumstance would you like others to pray for you to be delivered from evil?

Did You Get It? How has this week's study helped you see Satan's part in evil and our responsibility for evil?

Share with Someone: Think of a person you can encourage with the truth you learned in this session. Write their name in the space below and pray for God to provide that opportunity this week.

LIVING ON PURPOSE
Worship

The Bible tells us to *"overcome evil with good"* (Romans 12:21 NIV). The goodness of God helps us put the reality of evil in the proper perspective. Focus this week on the goodness of God by reading the following verses as you begin or end the day. Consider writing them out on cards so you can take them with you and read them throughout the day; or place them beside your bed and read them before you go to sleep.

For God is good, and he loves goodness; the godly shall see his face.
(Psalm 11:7 LB)

I am still confident of this: I will see the goodness of the LORD in the land of the living. (Psalm 27:13 NIV)

⁸Open your mouth and taste, open your eyes and see—how good GOD is. Blessed are you who run to him. ⁹Worship GOD if you want the best; worship opens doors to all his goodness. (Psalm 34:8-9 MSG)

The LORD is good to all; he has compassion on all he has made.
(Psalm 145:9 NIV)

The LORD is good, a refuge in times of trouble. He cares for those who trust in him. (Nahum 1:7 NIV)

. . . you are a chosen people. You are a kingdom of priests, God's holy nation, his very own possession. This is so you can show others the goodness of God, for he called you out of the darkness into his wonderful light. (1 Peter 2:9 NLT)

There's no particular virtue in accepting punishment that you well deserve. But if you're treated badly for good behavior and continue in spite of it to be a good servant, that is what counts with God.
(1 Peter 2:20 MSG)

PRAYER DIRECTION

Serve one another in love by praying for the needs expressed in your group today. Consider gathering around a group member who is experiencing a difficult time and laying hands on him or her while you pray for his or her needs.

3

Session three

VICTORY OVER EVIL—
OUR PART

CATCHING UP

1. What did you learn by focusing on God's goodness during last week's purpose activity? How did it change your perspective?

2. Did you notice that you were more aware of the Holy Spirit's presence in your life as a result of last week's lesson? Share any opportunities or insights you may have observed.

Key Verse

Submit yourselves, then, to God. Resist the devil, and he will flee from you.

James 4:7 (NIV)

BIBLE TEACHING
Watch the video lesson now and take notes in
your outline on pages 19–22.

Set Your Mind on Victory

*. . . everyone who is a child of God conquers the world. And
this is the victory that conquers the world—our faith.*
(1 John 5:4 NCV)

*God stripped the spiritual rulers and powers of their authority.
With the cross, he won the victory and showed the world that
they were powerless.* (Colossians 2:15 NCV)

*But we thank God! He gives us the victory through our Lord
Jesus Christ.* (1 Corinthians 15:57 NCV)

*. . . overwhelming victory is ours through Christ who loved us
enough to die for us.* (Romans 8:37 LB)

Be _____ .

- We live "_____ enemy lines."

  *[15]"My prayer is not that you take them out of the world but that
  you protect them from the evil one. [16]They are not of the world,
  even as I am not of it . . . . [18]As you sent me into the world, I
  have sent them into the world."* (John 17:15–16, 18 NIV)

- Satan is a "_____ lion."

  *Be self-controlled and alert. Your enemy the devil prowls
  around like a roaring lion looking for someone to devour.*
  (1 Peter 5:8 NIV)

Be _____ .

> [6b] *"God opposes the proud but gives grace to the humble."* [7]*Submit yourselves, then, to God. Resist the devil, and he will flee from you.* (James 4:6b–7 NIV)

- You start resisting Satan by _____ to God.

Be _____ .

- Confident because of God's _____

> *. . . the one who is in you is greater than the one who is in the world.* (1 John 4:4 NIV)

- Confident because of God's _____

> *The God of peace will soon crush Satan under your feet. The grace of our Lord Jesus be with you.* (Romans 16:20 NIV)

- Confident because of your _____

  Jesus told us to pray with faith for personal victory over evil.

> *"And lead us not into temptation, but deliver us from the evil one."* (Matthew 6:13 NIV)

Understand the Three Channels of Evil

The _____

"The world" means the philosophy and influence that reigns on this earth.

> *For everything in the world—the cravings of sinful man, the lust of his eyes and the boasting of what he has and does—comes not from the Father but from the world.* (1 John 2:16 NIV)

VICTORY OVER EVIL— OUR PART

Strategy for Victory

_____ the Lord.

> *¹⁵Do not love the world or anything in the world. If anyone loves the world, the love of the Father is not in him. ¹⁶For everything in the world—the cravings of sinful man, the lust of his eyes and the boasting of what he has and does—comes not from the Father but from the world. ¹⁷The world and its desires pass away, but the man who does the will of God lives forever.* (1 John 2:15–17 NIV)

The _____

A FRESH WORD

Flesh

There are two meanings for "flesh" in the Bible:

1. Our physical bodies (1 Corinthians 15:39; John 1:14)

2. Our spiritual *"disposition to sin"* (1 Corinthians 3:3 NASB)

This is important stuff! There is a huge difference between saying "our bodies are evil" and "our flesh is evil." Our bodies are meant to be temples of the Holy Spirit! First Corinthians 15 tells us that our bodies will one day be resurrected to eternal life. Sin starts in our unwilling hearts, not our physical bodies. Sin comes from the inside out rather than outside in. The heart is where the evil is. We don't think evil things because we live in an evil world; we live in an evil world because we think evil things! (Matthew 15:10-20)

Strategy for Victory

> *¹³You, my brothers, were called to be free. But do not use your freedom to indulge the sinful nature; rather, serve one another in love . . . . ¹⁶So I say, live by the Spirit, and you will not gratify the desires of the sinful nature.* (Galatians 5:13, 16 NIV)

_____ one another in love.

_____ by the Spirit.

The _____

Review the brief "biography" of Satan on page 11 of Session Two.

Strategy for Victory

Put on spiritual _____ .

> [13]*Therefore put on the full armor of God, so that when the day of evil comes, you may be able to stand your ground, and after you have done everything, to stand. *[14]*Stand firm then, with the belt of truth buckled around your waist, with the breastplate of righteousness in place, *[15]*and with your feet fitted with the readiness that comes from the gospel of peace. *[16]*In addition to all this, take up the shield of faith, with which you can extinguish all the flaming arrows of the evil one. *[17]*Take the helmet of salvation and the sword of the Spirit, which is the word of God. *[18]*And pray in the Spirit on all occasions with all kinds of prayers and requests. With this in mind, be alert and always keep on praying for all the saints.*
> (Ephesians 6:13–18 NIV)

What is this armor? Don't focus so much on the picture of belts and breastplates in Ephesians 6; focus on what the picture is communicating. Paul discusses seven things that are armor against the Devil's schemes:

1. Truth
2. Righteousness
3. Readiness to share the good news
4. Faith
5. Salvation
6. God's Word
7. Prayer

DISCOVERY QUESTIONS

1. The key truths shared in this session centered around ways to actively set our minds on the victory we have in Jesus. We are encouraged to be alert, humble, and confident. In which of these three areas would you like to begin to think in new ways?

2. As a group, how can you help one another experience victory over the world, the flesh, and the Evil One? How can you encourage each other as you face the daily reality of craving for possessions, lusting after passions, and boasting in pride?

3. Have you found one or more of the seven pieces of armor listed in Ephesians 6 to be effective in giving you protection from evil? In what ways? Discuss how you put on this armor in your daily life.

Did You Get It? In what ways has this week's study helped you see how to set your mind on victory?

Share with Someone: Think of a person you can encourage with the truth you learned in this session. Write their name in the space below and pray for God to provide that opportunity this week.

LIVING ON PURPOSE
Discipleship

Work on putting on the spiritual armor of God this next week. As you get dressed each day, dress spiritually by thinking through and mentally "putting on" each of the seven weapons of defense and offense against evil and for God's good.

PRAYER DIRECTION

Take a few minutes to thank God for providing ways for us to have victory over evil in this world. Praise him for his love, his Spirit, and his armor. Thank God for the specific pieces of armor protecting you right now.

Session four

4

VICTORY OVER EVIL—
GOD'S PART

CATCHING UP

1. What did you learn through "putting on" God's armor daily?

2. The strategy for victory over the influence of the world is to love the Lord. The strategy for victory over the flesh is to serve one another and live by the Spirit. And the strategy for victory over the Devil is putting on the spiritual armor of God. How did you do in applying these strategies since the last meeting? If your battle plan was weak, how can you strengthen it this next week?

3. One of the ways we grow spiritually is by passing along to others what we've learned. Did you have an opportunity to share with someone this last week about the three channels of evil? How did it go? What was their response?

Key Verse

Do not be overcome by evil, but overcome evil with good.

Romans 12:21 (NIV)

BIBLE TEACHING
Watch the video lesson now and take notes in your outline on pages 27–30.

Different Types of Evil

There are many ways that we must face the reality of evil in the choices and circumstances of our daily lives. How do I enjoy God's victory when I face these different types of evil in my life?

Sin

- We face evil because of our own _____ choice to sin.

  Jesus replied, "I tell you the truth, everyone who sins is a slave to sin." (John 8:34 NIV)

- For victory, decide to _____ .

  But if we confess our sins to God, he will keep his promise and do what is right: he will forgive us our sins and purify us from all our wrongdoing. (1 John 1:9 TEV)

Trials

- We face evil because we live in a _____ world.
- For victory, decide to _____ .

  ¹James, a servant of God and of the Lord Jesus Christ, To the twelve tribes scattered among the nations: Greetings. ²Consider it pure joy, my brothers, whenever you face trials of many kinds, ³because you know that the testing of your faith develops perseverance. ⁴Perseverance must finish its work so that you may be mature and complete, not lacking anything. (James 1:1–4 NIV)

Two reasons why God allows problems in our lives:

1) To develop _____ (James 1:1–4)

2) To enable _____

> *... comforts us in all our troubles, so that we can comfort those in any trouble with the comfort we ourselves have received from God.* (2 Corinthians 1:4 NIV)

Temptation

- We face evil because Satan _____ us to do wrong.
- For victory, decide to _____ .

Four truths to remember about temptation:

1) Temptation will always be a part of our lives.

2) It is not a sin to be tempted; it's a sin to give in to temptation.

3) We all face the same temptations.

> *These are the ways of the world: wanting to please our sinful selves, wanting the sinful things we see, and being too proud of what we have. None of these come from the Father, but all of them come from the world.* (1 John 2:16 NCV)

4) There is _____ a way of escape.

> *No temptation has seized you except what is common to man. And God is faithful; he will not let you be tempted beyond what you can bear. But when you are tempted, he will also provide a way out so that you can stand up under it.* (1 Corinthians 10:13 NIV)

A CLOSER LOOK
An Often Asked Question

How do you deal with a "habitual sin"—the cycle of sin, confess, sin, confess?

Change the pattern to "sin—confess—refocus."

Sometimes we become our own worst enemy. The more we focus on what we're not going to do, the more we're tempted by it and drawn into doing it. If you get into a tug-of-war with Satan, you'll lose! The solution: Drop your end of the rope and walk away. Refuse to play Satan's game.

Here are four ways to refocus your thinking:

1. _____

2. _____ departure

3. Tell the _____

4. _____ over time

Don't be discouraged if you do not feel an immediate change. Think of it as balancing a scale. As you continue to put weight on the positive side, one day the scales will tip.

The #1 Principle for Overcoming Evil

Take the offensive!

- When faced with inner accusation, picture the _____.

  ... God took away Satan's power to accuse you of sin, and God openly displayed to the whole world Christ's triumph at the cross where your sins were all taken away. (Colossians 2:15 LB)

- When faced with outer confrontation, picture yourself as

  _____ .

  [He] who gave himself for our sins to rescue us from the present evil age ... (Galatians 1:4 NIV)

- When faced with evil, do _____ .

  Do not be overcome by evil, but overcome evil with good.
  (Romans 12:21 NIV)

This extremely significant verse tells us how important our focus is. You'll never defeat evil by focusing on evil: Satan and demons and the evil forces of this world. Evil is defeated by focusing on what is good and living what is good.

> *. . . we come through all these things triumphantly victorious, by the power of him who loved us.* (Romans 8:37 NJB)

DISCOVERY QUESTIONS

1. Which area do you struggle with the most? Overcoming pride (the temptation to be), pleasure (the temptation to do), or possession (the temptation to have)? What tool or practice have you found most effective in dealing with personal temptation?

(Facing evil in our lives is inevitable, but the victory has already been won at the cross. For the following exercise we suggest you pair up with your spiritual partner for individual prayer and accountability.)

2. How can you overcome evil with good this week in each of the following areas?

One specific thought: How can you change your focus from what is evil to what is good in the way you think?

One specific habit: How can you change a bad habit by committing to a good habit?

One specific relationship: How can you begin to see what someone might have meant for evil as something God can use for good?

One specific problem: How can you rejoice in what God is doing in your life through a problem you are facing right now?

Did You Get It? How has this week's study helped you to see some personal choices you can make to overcome evil?

Share with Someone: Think of a person you can encourage with the truth you learned in this session. Write their name in the space below and pray for God to provide that opportunity this week.

LIVING ON PURPOSE

Ministry

Is there someone you know outside your group who is going through a time of suffering? What could your group do to help and encourage them?

PRAYER DIRECTION

Take some time as a group to talk about your specific prayer requests and to pray for one another. Thank God for his good and ultimate victory over evil.

Small Group Resources

HELPS FOR HOSTS

Top Ten Ideas for New Hosts

Congratulations! As the host of your small group, you have responded to the call to help shepherd Jesus' flock. Few other tasks in the family of God surpass the contribution you will be making.

As you prepare to facilitate your group, whether it is one session or the entire series, here are a few thoughts to keep in mind. We encourage you to read and review these tips with each new discussion host before he or she leads.

Remember you are not alone. God knows everything about you, and he knew you would be asked to facilitate your group. Even though you may not feel ready, this is common for all good hosts. God promises, *"I will never leave you; I will never abandon you"* (Hebrews 13:5 TEV). Whether you are facilitating for one evening, several weeks, or a lifetime, you will be blessed as you serve.

1. **Don't try to do it alone.** Pray right now for God to help you build a healthy team. If you can enlist a cohost to help you shepherd the group, you will find your experience much richer. This is your chance to involve as many people as you can in building a healthy group. All you have to do is ask people to help. You'll be surprised at the response.

2. **Be friendly and be yourself.** God wants to use your unique gifts and temperament. Be sure to greet people at the door with a big smile . . . this can set the mood for the whole gathering. Remember, they are taking as big a step to show up at your house as you are to lead this group! Don't try to do things exactly like another host; do them in a way that fits you. Admit when you don't have an answer and apologize when you make a mistake. Your group will love you for it and you'll sleep better at night.

3. **Prepare for your meeting ahead of time.** Review the session and write down your responses to each question. Pay special attention to exercises that ask group members to do something other than engage in discussion. These exercises will help your group live what the Bible teaches, not just talk about it. Be sure you understand how an exercise works. If the exercise employs one of the items in the Small Group Resources section (such as the Group Guidelines), be sure to look over that item so you'll know how it works.

4. **Pray for your group members by name.** Before you begin your session, take a few moments and pray for each member by name. You may want to review the prayer list at least once a week. Ask God to use your time together to touch the heart of every person in your group. Expect God to lead you to whomever he wants you to encourage or challenge in a special way. If you listen, God will surely lead.

5. **When you ask a question, be patient.** Someone will eventually respond. Sometimes people need a moment or two of silence to think about the question. If silence doesn't bother you, it won't bother anyone else. After someone responds, affirm the response with a simple "thanks" or "great answer." Then ask, "How about somebody else?" or "Would someone who hasn't shared like to add anything?" Be sensitive to new people or reluctant members who aren't ready to say, pray, or do anything. If you give them a safe setting, they will blossom over time. If someone in your group is a "wallflower" who sits silently through every session, consider talking to them privately and encouraging them to participate. Let them know how important they are to you—that they are loved and appreciated—and that the group would value their input. Remember, still water often runs deep.

6. **Provide transitions between questions.** Ask if anyone would like to read the paragraph or Bible passage. Don't call on anyone, but ask for a volunteer, and then be patient until someone begins. Be sure to thank the person who reads aloud.

7. **Break into smaller groups occasionally.** With a greater opportunity to talk in a small circle, people will connect more with the study, apply more quickly what they're learning, and ultimately get more out of their small group experience. A small circle also encourages a quiet person to participate and tends to minimize the effects of a more vocal or dominant member.

8. **Small circles are also helpful during prayer time.** People who are unaccustomed to praying aloud will feel more comfortable trying it with just two or three others. Also, prayer requests won't take as much time, so circles will have more time to actually pray. When you gather back with the whole group, you can have one person from each circle briefly update everyone on the prayer requests from their subgroups. The other great aspect of subgrouping is that it fosters leadership development. As you ask people in the group to facilitate discussion or to lead a prayer circle, it gives them a small leadership step that can build their confidence.

9. **Rotate facilitators occasionally.** You may be perfectly capable of hosting each time, but you will help others grow in their faith and gifts if you give them opportunities to host the group.

10. **One final challenge (for new or first-time hosts).** Before your first opportunity to lead, look up each of the six passages that follow. Read each one as a devotional exercise to help prepare you with a shepherd's heart. Trust us on this one. If you do this, you will be more than ready for your first meeting.

Matthew 9:36–38 (NIV)

36When Jesus saw the crowds, he had compassion on them, because they were harassed and helpless, like sheep without a shepherd. 37Then he said to his disciples, "The harvest is plentiful but the workers are few. 38Ask the Lord of the harvest, therefore, to send out workers into his harvest field."

John 10:14–15 (NIV)

14I am the good shepherd; I know my sheep and my sheep know me—15just as the Father knows me and I know the Father—and I lay down my life for the sheep.

1 Peter 5:2–4 (NIV)

²Be shepherds of God's flock that is under your care, serving as overseers—not because you must, but because you are willing, as God wants you to be; ³not greedy for money, but eager to serve; not lording it over those entrusted to you, but being examples to the flock. ⁴And when the Chief Shepherd appears, you will receive the crown of glory that will never fade away.

Philippians 2:1–5 (NIV)

¹If you have any encouragement from being united with Christ, if any comfort from his love, if any fellowship with the Spirit, if any tenderness and compassion, ²then make my joy complete by being like-minded, having the same love, being one in spirit and purpose. ³Do nothing out of selfish ambition or vain conceit, but in humility consider others better than yourselves. ⁴Each of you should look not only to your own interests, but also to the interests of others. ⁵Your attitude should be the same as that of Jesus Christ.

Hebrews 10:23–25 (NIV)

²³Let us hold unswervingly to the hope we profess, for he who promised is faithful. ²⁴And let us consider how we may spur one another on toward love and good deeds. ²⁵Let us not give up meeting together, as some are in the habit of doing, but let us encourage one another—and all the more as you see the Day approaching.

1 Thessalonians 2:7–8, 11–12 (NIV)

⁷. . . but we were gentle among you, like a mother caring for her little children. ⁸We loved you so much that we were delighted to share with you not only the gospel of God but our lives as well, because you had become so dear to us. . . . ¹¹For you know that we dealt with each of you as a father deals with his own children, ¹²encouraging, comforting and urging you to live lives worthy of God, who calls you into his kingdom and glory.

FREQUENTLY ASKED QUESTIONS

How long will this group meet?

This volume of *Foundations: Good and Evil* is four sessions long. We encourage your group to add a fifth session for a celebration. In your final session, each group member may decide if he or she desires to continue on for another study. At that time you may also want to do some informal evaluation, discuss your Group Guidelines, and decide which study you want to do next. We recommend you visit our website at **www.saddlebackresources.com** for more video-based small group studies.

Who is the host?

The host is the person who coordinates and facilitates your group meetings. In addition to a host, we encourage you to select one or more group members to lead your group discussions. Several other responsibilities can be rotated, including refreshments, prayer requests, worship, or keeping up with those who miss a meeting. Shared ownership in the group helps everybody grow.

Where do we find new group members?

Recruiting new members can be a challenge for groups, especially new groups with just a few people, or existing groups that lose a few people along the way. We encourage you to use the *Circles of Life* diagram on page 42 of this DVD study guide to brainstorm a list of people from your workplace, church, school, neighborhood, family, and so on. Then pray for the people on each member's list. Allow each member to invite several people from their list. Some groups fear that newcomers will interrupt the intimacy that members have built over time. However, groups that welcome newcomers generally gain strength with the infusion of new blood. Remember, the next person you add just might become a friend for eternity. Logistically, groups find different ways to add members. Some groups remain permanently open, while others choose to open periodically, such as at the beginning or end of a study. If your group becomes too large for easy, face-to-face conversations, you can subgroup, forming a second discussion group in another room.

How do we handle the child care needs in our group?

Child care needs must be handled very carefully. This is a sensitive issue. We suggest you seek creative solutions as a group. One common solution is to have the adults meet in the living room and share the cost of a babysitter (or two) who can be with the kids in another part of the house. Another popular option is to have one home for the kids and a second home (close by) for the adults. If desired, the adults could rotate the responsibility of providing a lesson for the kids. This last option is great with school-age kids and can be a huge blessing to families.

GROUP GUIDELINES

It's a good idea for every group to put words to their shared values, expectations, and commitments. Such guidelines will help you avoid unspoken agendas and unmet expectations. We recommend you discuss your guidelines during Session One in order to lay the foundation for a healthy group experience. Feel free to modify anything that does not work for your group.

We agree to the following values:

Clear Purpose	To grow healthy spiritual lives by building a healthy small group community
Group Attendance	To give priority to the group meeting (call if I am absent or late)
Safe Environment	To create a safe place where people can be heard and feel loved (no quick answers, snap judgments, or simple fixes)
Be Confidential	To keep anything that is shared strictly confidential and within the group
Conflict Resolution	To avoid gossip and to immediately resolve any concerns by following the principles of Matthew 18:15–17
Spiritual Health	To give group members permission to speak into my life and help me live a healthy, balanced spiritual life that is pleasing to God
Limit Our Freedom	To limit our freedom by not serving or consuming alcohol during small group meetings or events so as to avoid causing a weaker brother or sister to stumble (1 Corinthians 8:1–13; Romans 14:19–21)

Welcome Newcomers   To invite friends who might benefit from this study and warmly welcome newcomers

Building Relationships   To get to know the other members of the group and pray for them regularly

Other   _____

We have also discussed and agreed on the following items:

Child Care

_____

_____

Starting Time

_____

Ending Time

_____

If you haven't already done so, take a few minutes to fill out the *Small Group Calendar* on page 46.

CIRCLES OF LIFE—SMALL GROUP CONNECTIONS

Discover who you can connect in community

Use this chart to help carry out one of the values in the Group Guidelines, to "Welcome Newcomers."

"Follow me, and I will make you fishers of men." (Matthew 4:19 KJV)

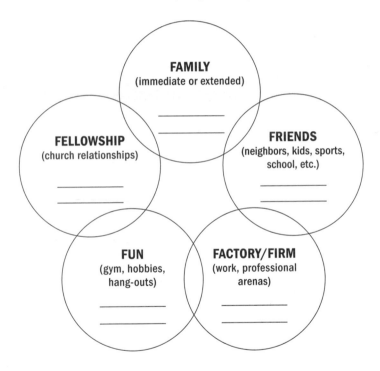

Follow this simple three-step process:

1. List 1–2 people in each circle.

2. Prayerfully select one person or couple from your list and tell your group about them.

3. Give them a call and invite them to your next meeting. Over 50 percent of those invited to a small group say, "Yes!"

SMALL GROUP PRAYER AND PRAISE REPORT

This is a place where you can write each other's requests for prayer. You can also make a note when God answers a prayer. Pray for each other's requests. If you're new to group prayer, it's okay to pray silently or to pray by using just one sentence: "God, please help

_____ to _____ ."

DATE	PERSON	PRAYER REQUEST	PRAISE REPORT

SMALL GROUP PRAYER AND PRAISE REPORT

DATE	PERSON	PRAYER REQUEST	PRAISE REPORT

SMALL GROUP PRAYER AND PRAISE REPORT

DATE	PERSON	PRAYER REQUEST	PRAISE REPORT

SMALL GROUP CALENDAR

Healthy groups share responsibilities and group ownership. It might take some time for this to develop. Shared ownership ensures that responsibility for the group doesn't fall to one person. Use the calendar to keep track of social events, mission projects, birthdays, or days off. Complete this calendar at your first or second meeting. Planning ahead will increase attendance and shared ownership.

DATE	LESSON	LOCATION	FACILITATOR	SNACK OR MEAL
5/4	Session 2	Chris and Andrea	Jim Brown	Phil and Karen

ANSWER KEY

Session One:
Why Evil Exists

1. God is <u>good</u>.
   - His <u>character</u> is good.
   - His <u>actions</u> are good.
2. God is <u>all-powerful</u>.
3. The world is <u>evil</u>.

There is no <u>love</u> without choice.

1) God is <u>sovereign</u>.
2) Mankind has <u>free</u> choice.

1. God's will: because God <u>allows</u> evil.

   - He made a world in which evil <u>could</u> exist.
   - God allows evil to <u>continue</u> to exist.

   1. He directly <u>causes</u> some suffering.
   2. He has <u>compassion</u> for all suffering.
   3. He is willing to <u>care</u> for us in our suffering.
   4. He develops our <u>character</u> through suffering.
   5. He will one day <u>cease</u> all suffering.

Session Two:
Satan's Influence—Man's Choice

2. Satan's influence: because Satan <u>afflicts</u> evil.

   - He was an <u>angel</u> in heaven.
   - He <u>fell</u> from heaven due to pride.
   - He has been given <u>limited</u> freedom to influence the earth.

   Satan's limit: he must ask <u>God's permission</u>.

   - He is unalterably <u>condemned</u> to eternal destruction.

3. Mankind's choice: because we <u>accept</u> evil.

   Evil began with <u>them</u>.
   Evil is present in <u>me</u>.

   - He already has <u>defeated</u> evil.
   - He is <u>patient</u>.

Session Three:
Victory over Evil—Our Part

Be _alert_.
   - We live "<u>behind</u> enemy lines."
   - Satan is a "<u>roaring</u> lion."

Be _humble_.
   - You start resisting Satan by <u>submitting</u> to God.

Be _confident_.
   - Confident because of God's <u>presence</u>
   - Confident because of God's <u>promise</u>
   - Confident because of your <u>prayers</u>

The _world_
<u>Love</u> the Lord.

The _flesh_
<u>Serve</u> one another in love.
<u>Live</u> by the Spirit.

The _Devil_
Put on spiritual <u>armor</u>.

Session Four:
Victory over Evil—God's Part

   - We face evil because of our own personal choice to sin.
   - For victory, decide to <u>repent</u>.

   - We face evil because we live in a <u>fallen</u> world.
   - For victory, decide to <u>rejoice</u>.

1) To develop <u>maturity</u>
2) To enable <u>ministry</u>

   - We face evil because Satan <u>tempts</u> us to do wrong.
   - For victory, decide to <u>reject</u>.

4) There is <u>always</u> a way of escape.

1. <u>Worship</u>
2. <u>Radical</u> departure
3. Tell the <u>truth</u>
4. <u>Faithfulness</u> over time

   - When faced with inner accusation, picture the <u>cross</u>.
   - When faced with outer confrontation, picture yourself as <u>rescued</u>.
   - When faced with evil, do <u>good</u>.

NOTES

KEY VERSES

One of the most effective ways to drive deeply into our lives the principles we are learning in this series is to memorize key Scriptures. For many, memorization is a new concept or one that has been difficult in the past. We encourage you to stretch yourself and try to memorize these four key verses. If possible, memorize these as a group and make them part of your group time. You may cut these apart and carry them in your wallet.

I have hidden your word in my heart that I might not sin against you.

Psalm 119:11 (NIV)

Session One *For the LORD is good and his love endures forever; his faithfulness continues through all generations.* Psalm 100:5 (NIV)	**Session Two** *. . . for all have sinned and fall short of the glory of God . . .* Romans 3:23 (NIV)
Session Three *Submit yourselves, then, to God. Resist the devil, and he will flee from you . . .* James 4:7 (NIV)	**Session Four** *Do not be overcome by evil, but overcome evil with good.* Romans 12:21 (NIV)

NOTES

We value your thoughts about what you've just read.
Please share them with us. You'll find contact information
in the back of this book.

The Purpose Driven® Life
A six-session video-based study for groups or individuals

Embark on a journey of discovery with this video-based study taught by Rick Warren. In it you will discover the answer to life's most fundamental question: "What on earth am I here for?"

And here's a clue to the answer: "It's not about you . . . You were created by God and for God, and until you understand that, life will never make sense. It is only in God that we discover our origin, our identity, our meaning, our purpose, our significance, and our destiny."

Whether you experience this adventure with a small group or on your own, this six-session, video-based study will change your life.

DVD Study Guide: 978-0-310-27866-5
DVD: 978-0-310-27864-1

Be sure to combine this study with your reading of the best-selling book, *The Purpose Driven® Life,* to give you or your small group the opportunity to discuss the implications and applications of living the life God created you to live.

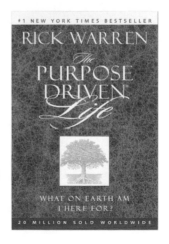

Hardcover, Jacketed: 978-0-310-20571-5
Softcover: 978-0-310-27699-9

Pick up a copy today at your favorite bookstore!

Foundations: 11 Core Truths to Build Your Life On

Taught by Tom Holladay and Kay Warren

Foundations is a series of 11 four-week video studies covering the most important, foundational doctrines of the Christian faith. Study topics include:

The Bible—This study focuses on where the Bible came from, why it can be trusted, and how it can change your life.

DVD Study Guide: 978-0-310-27670-8
DVD: 978-0-310-27669-2

God—This study focuses not just on facts about God, but on how to know God himself in a more powerful and personal way.

DVD Study Guide: 978-0-310-27672-2
DVD: 978-0-310-27671-5

Jesus—As we look at what the Bible says about the person of Christ, we do so as people who are developing a lifelong relationship with Jesus.

DVD Study Guide: 978-0-310-27674-6
DVD: 978-0-310-27673-9

The Holy Spirit—This study focuses on the person, the presence, and the power of the Holy Spirit, and how you can be filled with the Holy Spirit on a daily basis.

DVD Study Guide: 978-0-310-27676-0
DVD: 978-0-310-27675-3

Creation—Each of us was personally created by a loving God. This study does not shy away from the great scientific and theological arguments that surround the creation/evolution debate. However, you will find the goal of this study is deepening your awareness of God as your Creator.

DVD Study Guide: 978-0-310-27678-4
DVD: 978-0-310-27677-7

Pick up a copy today at your favorite bookstore!

Salvation—This study focuses on God's solution to man's need for salvation, what Jesus Christ did for us on the cross, and the assurance and security of God's love and provision for eternity.

DVD Study Guide: 978-0-310-27682-1
DVD: 978-0-310-27679-1

Sanctification—This study focuses on the two natures of the Christian. We'll see the difference between grace and law, and how these two things work in our lives.

DVD Study Guide: 978-0-310-27684-5
DVD: 978-0-310-27683-8

Good and Evil—Why do bad things happen to good people? Through this study we'll see how and why God continues to allow evil to exist. The ultimate goal is to build up our faith and relationship with God as we wrestle with these difficult questions.

DVD Study Guide: 978-0-310-27687-6
DVD: 978-0-310-27686-9

The Afterlife—The Bible does not answer all the questions we have about what happens to us after we die; however, this study deals with what the Bible does tell us. This important study gives us hope and helps us move from a focus on the here and now to a focus on eternity.

DVD Study Guide: 978-0-310-27689-0
DVD: 978-0-310-27688-3

The Church—This study focuses on the birth of the church, the nature of the church, and the mission of the church.

DVD Study Guide: 978-0-310-27692-0
DVD: 978-0-310-27691-3

The Second Coming—This study addresses both the hope and the uncertainties surrounding the second coming of Jesus Christ.

DVD Study Guide: 978-0-310-27695-1
DVD: 978-0-310-27693-7

Pick up a copy today at your favorite bookstore!

ZONDERVAN®
.com

Celebrate Recovery, Updated Curriculum Kit

This kit will provide your church with the tools necessary to start a successful Celebrate Recovery program. *Kit includes:*

- Introductory Guide for Leaders DVD
- Leader's Guide
- 4 Participant's Guides (one of each guide)
- CD-ROM with 25 lessons
- CD-ROM with sermon transcripts
- 4-volume audio CD sermon series

Curriculum Kit: 978-0-310-26847-5

Participant's Guide 4-pack

The Celebrate Recovery Participant's Guide 4-pack is a convenient resource when you're just getting started or if you need replacement guides for your program.

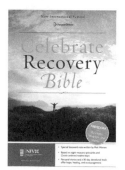

Celebrate Recovery Bible

With features based on eight principles Jesus voiced in his Sermon on the Mount, the new *Celebrate Recovery Bible* offers hope, encouragement, and empowerment for those struggling with the circumstances of their lives and the habits they are trying to control.

Hardcover: 978-0-310-92849-2
Softcover: 978-0-310-93810-1

Pick up a copy today at your favorite bookstore!

ZONDERVAN®
.com

Small Group Leadership Tools

Stepping Out of Denial into God's Grace

Participant's Guide 1 introduces the eight principles of recovery based on Jesus' words in the Beatitudes, and focuses on principles 1–3. Participants learn about denial, hope, sanity, and more.

Getting Right with God, Yourself, and Others

Participant's Guide 3 covers principles 5–7 based on Jesus' words in the Beatitudes. With courage and support from their fellow participants, people seeking recovery will find victory, forgiveness, and grace.

Taking an Honest and Spiritual Inventory

Participant's Guide 2 focuses on the fourth principle based on Jesus' words in the Beatitudes and builds on the Scripture, *"Happy are the pure in heart."* (Matthew 5:8) The participant will learn an invaluable principle for recovery and also take an in-depth spiritual inventory.

Growing in Christ While Helping Others

Participant's Guide 4 walks through the final steps of the eight recovery principles based on Jesus' words in the Beatitudes. In this final phase, participants learn to move forward in newfound freedom in Christ, learning how to give back to others. There's even a practical lesson called "Seven reasons we get stuck in our recoveries."

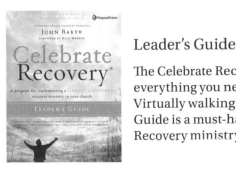

Leader's Guide

The Celebrate Recovery Leader's Guide gives you everything you need to facilitate your preparation time. Virtually walking you through every meeting, the Leader's Guide is a must-have for every leader on your Celebrate Recovery ministry team.

Pick up a copy today at your favorite bookstore!

Wide Angle:
Framing Your Worldview

Christianity is much more than a religion. It is a worldview—a way of seeing all of life and the world around you. Your worldview impacts virtually every decision you make in life: moral decisions, relational decisions, financial decisions—everything. How you see the world determines how you face the world.

In this brand new study, Rick Warren and Chuck Colson discuss such key issues as moral relativism, tolerance, terrorism, creationism vs. Darwinism, sin and suffering. They explore in depth the Christian worldview as it relates to the most important questions in life:

- Why does it matter what I believe?
- How do I know what's true?
- Where do I come from?
- Why is the world so messed up?
- Is there a solution?
- What is my purpose in life?

Rick Warren   *Chuck Colson*

This study is as deep as it is wide, addressing vitally important topics for every follower of Christ.

DVD Study Guide: 978-1-4228-0083-6
DVD: 978-1-4228-0082-9

The Way of a Worshiper

The pursuit of God is the chase of a lifetime—in fact, it's been going on since the day you were born. The question is: Have you been the hunter or the prey?

This small group study is not about music. It's not even about going to church. It's about living your life as an offering of worship to God. It's about tapping into the source of power to live the Christian life. And it's about discovering the secret to friendship with God.

In these four video sessions, Buddy Owens helps you unpack the meaning 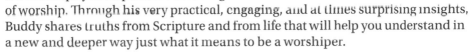 of worship. Through his very practical, engaging, and at times surprising insights, Buddy shares truths from Scripture and from life that will help you understand in a new and deeper way just what it means to be a worshiper.

God is looking for worshipers. His invitation to friendship is open and genuine. Will you take him up on his offer? Will you give yourself to him in worship? Then come walk *The Way of a Worshiper* and discover the secret to friendship with God.

DVD Study Guide: 978-1-4228-0096-6
DVD: 978-1-4228-0095-9

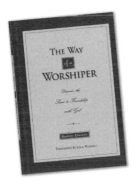

THE WAY of a WORSHIPER

Your study of this material will be greatly enhanced by reading the book, *The Way of a Worshiper: Discover the Secret to Friendship with God.*

Managing Our Finances God's Way

Did you know that there are over 2,350 verses in the Bible about money? Did you know that nearly half of Jesus' parables are about possessions? The Bible is packed with wise counsel about your financial life. In fact, Jesus had more to say about money than about heaven and hell combined.

Introducing a new video-based small group study that will inspire you to live debt free! Created by Saddleback Church and Crown Financial Ministries, learn what the Bible has to say about our finances from Rick Warren, Chip Ingram, Ron Blue, Howard Dayton, and Chuck Bentley as they address important topics like:

- God's Solution to Debt
- Saving and Investing
- Plan Your Spending
- Giving as an Act of Worship
- Enjoy What God Has Given You

Study includes:

- DVD with seven 20-minute lessons

- Workbook with seven lessons

- Resource CD with digital version of all worksheets that perform calculations automatically

- Contact information for help with answering questions

- Resources for keeping financial plans on track and making them lifelong habits

> **NOTE:** PARTICIPANTS DO NOT SHARE PERSONAL FINANCIAL INFORMATION WITH EACH OTHER.

DVD Study Guide: 978-1-4228-0083-6
DVD: 978-1-4228-0082-9

Share Your Thoughts

With the Author: Your comments will be forwarded to the author when you send them to *zauthor@zondervan.com*.

With Zondervan: Submit your review of this book by writing to *zreview@zondervan.com*.

Free Online Resources at

www.zondervan.com/hello

 Zondervan AuthorTracker: Be notified whenever your favorite authors publish new books, go on tour, or post an update about what's happening in their lives.

 Daily Bible Verses and Devotions: Enrich your life with daily Bible verses or devotions that help you start every morning focused on God.

 Free Email Publications: Sign up for newsletters on fiction, Christian living, church ministry, parenting, and more.

 Zondervan Bible Search: Find and compare Bible passages in a variety of translations at www.zondervanbiblesearch.com.

 Other Benefits: Register yourself to receive online benefits like coupons and special offers, or to participate in research.